THE POWER OF RISK

The Untold Secrets of Risk and Reward

Lucas D. Harrington

Table of Contents

Chapter 1: THE NATURE OF RISK 4

Chapter 2: RISK AND REWARD: A DELICATE BALANCE 12

Chapter 3: THE PSYCHOLOGY OF RISK-TAKING 21

Chapter 4: CALCULATED RISK VS. RECKLESS RISK 31

Chapter 5: THE ROLE OF UNCERTAINTY 42

Chapter 6: RISK IN BUSINESS AND ENTREPRENEURSHIP 51

Chapter 7: FINANCIAL RISK AND REWARD 61

Chapter 8: RISK AND PERSONAL GROWTH 69

Chapter 9: MANAGING RISK IN A RELATIONSHIP 76

Chapter 10: MITIGATING RISK: STRATEGIES AND TOOLS 83

Chapter 11: THE COST OF AVOIDING RISK 91

Chapter 12: RISK-TAKING IN LEADERSHIP 100

Chapter 13: MASTERING THE ART OF RISK 109

CONCLUSION 120

References 124

About the Author 129

Disclaimer: 131

Copyright 132

Legal Notice 133

Chapter 1: THE NATURE OF RISK

Risk is one of the most fundamental aspects of human experience, yet it is often misunderstood. In every decision we make, from the most mundane daily choices to life-altering commitments, risk plays a pivotal role. Understanding what risk truly means—and how it operates in both our personal and professional lives—can transform the way we approach challenges and opportunities.

Risk: What Does It Really Mean?

At its core, risk is the potential for loss or harm, combined with the uncertainty of an outcome. The moment we leave the comfort of certainty, we enter a space where risk exists. This uncertainty creates both the possibility of reward and the fear of failure. Risk isn't simply about making a reckless or hasty decision—it's about weighing the potential costs and benefits of an action, knowing that there are no guarantees.

In both personal and professional settings, risk can manifest in a variety of ways. For some, it may be a career decision, like leaving a stable job to pursue entrepreneurship. For others, it might be a more personal choice, such as investing time and effort in a relationship or moving to a new city without a safety net. In each scenario, risk is not just a byproduct of the decision—it is the decision. The act of embracing the unknown requires courage and often a deep understanding of one's values, priorities, and desired outcomes.

The key to understanding risk is recognizing that it exists on a spectrum. Not all risks are equal; they vary in scale, impact, and likelihood. Some are calculated risks, where potential outcomes are carefully considered and managed, while others are high-stakes, uncertain ventures with potentially life-changing results. By acknowledging the different types of risks and their implications, we can begin to make more informed, deliberate choices.

The Different Forms of Risk

Risk can take many forms, and each type presents unique challenges. These forms can be broadly categorized into financial risk, emotional risk, social risk, and physical risk.

- Financial Risk: This is perhaps the most easily identifiable form of risk, often associated with investments, business ventures, or major purchases. It involves the potential loss of money, assets, or future earning potential. For individuals, financial risk might mean investing in the stock market, starting a business, or purchasing a home. For businesses, it could involve expansion efforts, mergers, or product launches. In both cases, the central question is whether the potential rewards outweigh the possible losses.

- Emotional Risk: While often overlooked, emotional risk is one of the most personal and profound types of risk. It involves vulnerability—putting oneself in situations that could lead to emotional pain, rejection, or disappointment. In relationships, emotional risk is present when we open ourselves up to love, friendship, or deep connections, knowing full well that those connections could lead to heartache. In professional settings, emotional risk might come from presenting an innovative idea or making a bold suggestion, fearing it will be criticized or rejected.
- Social Risk: Humans are social beings, and our standing within our communities or peer groups can carry significant weight. Social risk involves actions that could jeopardize one's reputation, standing, or social capital. Whether it's taking a public stance on a controversial issue, challenging a popular opinion, or pursuing a path

that defies societal norms, social risk can be intimidating. The fear of ostracization, ridicule, or disapproval often prevents people from taking socially risky actions, even when the potential benefits are substantial.

- Physical Risk: This is the most tangible form of risk, as it involves the potential for harm to one's physical well-being. Physical risk is present in activities such as extreme sports, adventure travel, or even manual labor. However, it's not limited to these arenas. Physical risk also appears in decisions related to health—such as undergoing a medical procedure or experimenting with a new diet or fitness regimen. It is the risk of injury, illness, or physical strain that defines this category.

Psychological Factors Influencing Risk-Taking

The willingness to take risks varies significantly from person to person. Some individuals seem to thrive in risky situations, relishing the adrenaline and excitement that come from uncertainty. Others are far more cautious, preferring the safety of predictability. What accounts for these differences?

A variety of psychological factors play a role in shaping how we perceive and approach risk. One key factor is risk tolerance—the degree to which a person is comfortable with uncertainty. Those with high risk tolerance are more likely to engage in behaviors that others might consider reckless or imprudent, but they see these actions as opportunities for growth, learning, or reward. In contrast, individuals with low risk tolerance tend to avoid uncertainty, seeking stability and security even at the cost of potential gains.

Risk tolerance is influenced by several factors, including personality, upbringing, and past experiences. For example, individuals who were encouraged to take calculated risks in their childhood, such as trying new sports or taking on leadership roles, may develop a higher tolerance for uncertainty as adults. Conversely, those who experienced significant negative consequences from risky behaviors may become more risk-averse.

Another factor is loss aversion, a concept from behavioral economics that refers to the tendency of people to prefer avoiding losses rather than acquiring equivalent gains. In other words, the pain of losing something is more powerful than the joy of gaining something of equal value. This cognitive bias can lead individuals to shy away from risks, even when the potential rewards are significant.

Overconfidence is another psychological element that influences risk-taking. Some individuals, particularly those who have experienced repeated success, may become overconfident in their ability to predict outcomes or control situations. This can lead to taking on unnecessary or poorly calculated risks, as the individual underestimates the likelihood of failure. While confidence can be a valuable asset in risk-taking, overconfidence can lead to disaster if not tempered by careful consideration.

Fear also plays a critical role in risk assessment. Fear of failure, rejection, or loss can paralyze a person, preventing them from seizing opportunities or making bold moves. Fear can also distort perception, making a situation seem more perilous than it actually is. However, fear isn't always a hindrance. When managed properly, fear can act as a motivator, pushing individuals to prepare thoroughly, assess risks carefully, and avoid reckless behavior.

Risk in Personal and Professional Contexts

In personal life, risk is often tied to major life decisions—choosing a partner, starting a family, moving to a new location, or switching careers. These decisions are fraught with uncertainty, and the outcomes can be life-altering. However, without taking these risks, personal growth can be stunted, and opportunities for happiness and fulfillment can be missed. The decision to take a risk in one's personal life often comes down to a careful balance between fear and hope—fear of what could go wrong, and hope for what could go right.

In the professional realm, risk is intrinsic to success. Whether it's launching a new product, entering an unfamiliar market, or taking on a leadership role, professional growth is often predicated on the ability to take strategic risks. However, in the corporate world, risk is often calculated and managed with far more rigor. Professionals use tools like cost-benefit analysis, market research, and scenario planning to mitigate risks and increase the likelihood of success. Even so, no amount of preparation can eliminate risk entirely. The challenge is to embrace it as part of the process.

The nature of risk is complex, multifaceted, and deeply ingrained in the human experience. It is neither inherently good nor bad but simply a reality of life.

In both personal and professional contexts, risk is essential for growth, innovation, and fulfillment. Avoiding risk altogether may lead to safety and stability, but it also limits potential. Embracing risk, on the other hand, opens doors to new opportunities, experiences, and rewards.

Chapter 2: RISK AND REWARD: A DELICATE BALANCE

The relationship between risk and reward is at the heart of every significant decision we make. Whether in personal life, career, or business, we are constantly faced with choices that carry potential risks but also the promise of rewards. Understanding how these two forces are intertwined—and how to effectively manage the balance between them—is crucial for anyone seeking success and growth.

The Fundamental Principle: No Reward Without Risk

At its most basic level, risk is the exposure to uncertainty, while reward represents the potential positive outcome of an action. The two are inseparable. The greater the reward we seek, the more risk we typically have to accept. This principle is evident in countless areas of life, from investing money to making life decisions. People who are willing to accept a higher degree of uncertainty often find themselves in positions to reap greater rewards, but they also face a higher chance of failure.

This dynamic becomes apparent when we consider some common examples. Take, for instance, an entrepreneur launching a startup. There's a significant amount of risk involved—financial uncertainty, potential market rejection, and the possibility of personal failure. However, the potential reward is equally great—success in the form of financial freedom, personal fulfillment, and business growth. On the other hand, someone working in a stable job with a predictable salary may face minimal risk but also experiences limited opportunities for high-reward outcomes.

The principle that "there is no reward without risk" does not mean that we should dive into every risky situation. Instead, it means that we must be prepared to accept a certain level of uncertainty if we hope to achieve significant rewards. The challenge is to identify which risks are worth taking, which are unnecessary, and how to manage risk effectively so that it doesn't undermine our long-term success.

The Concept of Calculated Risk

While it may be true that no reward comes without risk, not all risks are created equal. Some risks are reckless and lead to disaster, while others are carefully calculated and increase the odds of success. The key to navigating this balance is learning how to evaluate and manage calculated risks.

A calculated risk is one that has been thoughtfully considered, with an understanding of both the potential rewards and the possible consequences. This type of risk is not taken on impulse but is supported by research, analysis, and a clear sense of purpose. When taking a calculated risk, the person or organization has a thorough understanding of the probabilities involved and has made preparations for various outcomes.

Take the example of an investor in the stock market. An experienced investor doesn't simply throw money at high-risk stocks on a whim. Instead, they assess the company's performance, industry trends, and economic conditions. They diversify their portfolio to mitigate risk and avoid putting all their resources into a single venture. By doing so, they increase their chances of earning a high return while reducing the likelihood of catastrophic losses. This is calculated risk in action.

In personal life, calculated risks might involve decisions like moving to a new city for a better job opportunity, investing in a passion project, or even taking on a challenging personal goal, like running a marathon. Each of these actions involves risk, but the potential rewards can be life-changing. By carefully considering factors such as timing, preparation, and long-term impact, these risks become more manageable and far more likely to lead to positive outcomes.

Assessing Risk: Is the Reward Worth It?

One of the most important skills in managing risk and reward is the ability to assess whether a risk is worth taking. This requires not only an understanding of the potential benefits but also an honest evaluation of the possible downsides. Here are some key questions to consider when determining whether a risk is worth it:

- What are the potential rewards? Before taking a risk, it's essential to have a clear idea of what the potential payoff might be. This could be financial gain, personal growth, career advancement, or some other form of success. The greater the reward, the more risk might be acceptable. For instance, starting your own business could lead to financial independence, while a risky investment might bring substantial returns. However, it's important to ensure that the reward is meaningful and aligns with your values and goals.

- What are the potential consequences? Every risk carries the potential for failure. Assessing the possible negative outcomes is crucial to making an informed decision. What are you prepared to lose if things don't go as planned? This could range from financial loss to damaged relationships, missed opportunities, or even harm to your reputation. Understanding what's at stake allows you to prepare contingency plans and avoid being blindsided if things go wrong.

- How likely is success? It's not enough to simply know the potential reward and the possible consequences—you also need to understand the likelihood of success. This is where research, data, and past experience come into play. Analyzing market trends, studying similar past ventures, and seeking advice from experts can help you determine how likely it is that your risk will pay off.

- Can the risk be mitigated? Not all risks are equally dangerous. Some risks can be reduced through planning and strategy. For example, a business owner may reduce the risk of failure by conducting market research, securing additional funding, or forming strategic partnerships. In personal life, risks might be mitigated by gathering support from friends and family, setting realistic timelines, or gaining new skills. Understanding how to reduce risk increases the odds of success.

The delicate balance between risk and reward lies in being able to honestly assess these factors. The goal is not to eliminate risk but to manage it effectively and make informed decisions that increase the probability of achieving the desired rewards.

The Role of Time in Risk and Reward

Time is a crucial factor in determining the balance between risk and reward. Short-term risks may offer immediate rewards but often come with higher stakes, while long-term risks allow for more strategic planning and a gradual approach to reaping benefits.

In the world of investing, short-term high-risk ventures, like day trading or investing in volatile stocks, can lead to quick gains but are also prone to significant losses. Long-term investments, such as real estate or retirement savings, tend to carry lower risk and provide more reliable returns, though the rewards take years or even decades to materialize.

Similarly, in personal development, short-term risks, like taking on a high-pressure project or learning a new skill quickly, may lead to immediate challenges and stress but also offer rapid personal growth. On the other hand, long-term risks, like pursuing higher education or starting a passion project, take more time to produce tangible results but can have a profound, lasting impact on one's life.

Balancing short-term and long-term risk is essential. While immediate rewards may be tempting, it's important to consider how short-term decisions align with your long-term goals. In many cases, the best strategy is to take a mix of both short- and long-term risks, allowing you to enjoy some immediate benefits while setting yourself up for future success.

The Psychology of Risk and Reward

The balance between risk and reward is not just a matter of logic and strategy—it is also deeply influenced by psychology. Our emotions, biases, and past experiences play a significant role in how we assess risks and rewards.

For many people, the fear of failure or loss can prevent them from taking any risk, even when the potential rewards far outweigh the possible downsides. This fear is often tied to a psychological phenomenon known as **loss aversion**, which refers to the tendency to fear losing something more than we value gaining something of equal worth. Loss aversion can skew our perception of risk, making even small risks seem disproportionately threatening.

On the flip side, some individuals may be overly **risk-seeking**, driven by the thrill of the unknown or the excitement of a potential big payoff. These people are often susceptible to overconfidence, which can cloud judgment and lead to reckless decisions. Overconfidence leads individuals to underestimate the likelihood of negative outcomes and to take on risks without adequate preparation.

Understanding the psychological factors that influence our relationship with risk and reward is essential for developing a balanced approach. By acknowledging biases like loss aversion and overconfidence, we can take a more objective view of risks and make decisions based on rational analysis rather than emotional reactions.

The delicate balance between risk and reward is not a one-size-fits-all equation. It requires careful assessment, preparation, and self-awareness. Whether in personal life, career, or business, those who can effectively evaluate the potential rewards of a risk against its possible consequences are better equipped to seize opportunities while minimizing negative outcomes.

The goal of mastering the balance of risk and reward is not to eliminate fear or uncertainty but to learn how to use them to your advantage. By taking calculated risks, preparing for different outcomes, and managing emotions, individuals can unlock the potential for significant growth and success in all areas of life.

Chapter 3: THE PSYCHOLOGY OF RISK-TAKING

Risk-taking is an inherent part of human nature. Whether in personal, professional, or financial arenas, we constantly weigh the potential rewards of our actions against the uncertainties and dangers involved. However, the decision to take a risk is often driven not purely by logic but by a complex interplay of emotions, mental processes, and cognitive biases. Understanding the psychology behind risk-taking is essential for anyone looking to make sound decisions, especially when the stakes are high.

The Role of Emotion in Risk-Taking

When it comes to risky decisions, emotions are often the driving force behind our actions. They can propel us to take a bold leap or paralyze us with fear, leading to indecision. Three primary emotions tend to dominate the risk-taking process: fear, excitement, and overconfidence. Each of these emotions can affect how we perceive risk, and each requires careful management to avoid making impulsive or irrational decisions.

1. Fear: The Paralyzing Force

Fear is perhaps the most common and powerful emotion associated with risk-taking. Fear of failure, fear of losing money, fear of embarrassment, or fear of the unknown can significantly impact our willingness to take risks. Fear often prevents us from taking action, even when the potential reward far outweighs the risk. This phenomenon is commonly referred to as risk aversion—the tendency to avoid risks in favor of safety and security.

At its core, fear is a protective mechanism. It keeps us from engaging in reckless behavior and helps us avoid situations that may result in harm or loss. However, fear can also be irrational, leading us to perceive risk as greater than it actually is. When fear clouds our judgment, we may become overly cautious, passing up valuable opportunities for growth and success.

The key to managing fear in risk-taking is to acknowledge it without allowing it to dictate our decisions. The first step is to recognize when fear is driving our behavior. Are you avoiding a particular course of action because you've logically determined it's too risky, or are you being held back by an emotional response? Once you identify fear's influence, you can take steps to mitigate it.

One effective strategy is to break down the risk into smaller, more manageable components. By analyzing each aspect of the risk and understanding the potential consequences, you can reduce uncertainty and make the situation feel less intimidating. Additionally, focusing on the potential rewards rather than the possible losses can help shift your perspective from fear to opportunity. Ultimately, fear should be respected as a natural part of risk-taking, but it should never be the sole determining factor in your decision-making process.

2. Excitement: The Thrill of the Unknown

On the other side of the emotional spectrum is excitement—a feeling that can often override caution and lead to impulsive risk-taking. For some, the allure of potential success or the adrenaline rush of uncertainty can be intoxicating, pushing them to take bigger and bolder risks than they would under normal circumstances. Excitement can be a powerful motivator, encouraging innovation, creativity, and breakthrough achievements. However, when unchecked, it can also lead to reckless behavior and poor decision-making.

People who are prone to high levels of excitement in the face of risk often engage in risk-seeking behavior, meaning they are more likely to pursue risky opportunities without fully considering the consequences. This can manifest in various ways, such as making impulsive financial investments, jumping into business ventures without proper planning, or taking unnecessary personal risks.

While excitement can fuel bold moves, it is important to temper it with rational thinking and thorough analysis. Before diving headfirst into a risky situation, take the time to assess whether your excitement is clouding your judgment. Ask yourself whether you've considered all possible outcomes and whether the potential rewards justify the risks. By balancing excitement with careful evaluation, you can channel that energy into calculated risks that are more likely to result in success.

3. Overconfidence: The Illusion of Control

Overconfidence is another common psychological pitfall in risk-taking. When we are overconfident, we tend to overestimate our abilities and underestimate the potential challenges or dangers associated with a risk. This cognitive bias can lead us to take on more risk than is warranted because we believe we have control over the outcome or that we are uniquely capable of succeeding where others have failed.

Overconfidence often stems from past successes. When things have gone well in previous risk-taking endeavors, we may start to believe that we are immune to failure. This mindset can be especially dangerous in fields like investing, entrepreneurship, or high-stakes decision-making, where external factors beyond our control—such as market conditions, economic shifts, or unforeseen circumstances—can significantly impact outcomes.

The key to avoiding overconfidence is self-awareness. Recognize that no matter how skilled or experienced you are, there are always elements of risk that you cannot control. It's essential to approach each risk with humility, understanding that success is never guaranteed. Seeking input from others, conducting thorough research, and planning for various contingencies are all ways to ensure that your confidence is based on reality rather than illusion.

The Cognitive Biases That Shape Risk Perception

Beyond emotions, our perception of risk is heavily influenced by cognitive biases—mental shortcuts that help us make decisions quickly but can also lead to errors in judgment. Cognitive biases affect how we interpret information, assess probabilities, and weigh risks and rewards. Understanding these biases can help you recognize when your decision-making is being skewed and allow you to correct course before making a risky decision.

1. Loss Aversion: The Fear of Losing

One of the most well-known cognitive biases is loss aversion, which refers to the tendency to fear losses more than we value equivalent gains. In other words, the pain of losing something is typically more intense than the pleasure of gaining something of the same value. Loss aversion often leads people to avoid taking risks, even when the potential reward is substantial.

For example, an investor may avoid a high-reward investment opportunity because they are too focused on the possibility of losing money, despite the fact that the probability of a positive outcome outweighs the risk of loss. Loss aversion can prevent us from pursuing opportunities that could lead to significant growth, both personally and professionally.

To overcome loss aversion, it's important to shift your focus from what you might lose to what you stand to gain. Reframe the situation by considering the potential upside and evaluating whether the risk is truly as great as it seems. Additionally, developing a mindset of resilience—where failure is viewed as a learning experience rather than a catastrophe—can help reduce the fear of loss and make you more willing to take calculated risks.

2. The Availability Heuristic: The Power of Recent Experiences

The availability heuristic is a cognitive bias that leads us to base our judgments on information that is readily available, such as recent experiences or highly memorable events. When it comes to risk-taking, the availability heuristic can cause us to overestimate the likelihood of negative outcomes if we've recently experienced or heard about a failure. Conversely, it can lead us to underestimate risk if we've recently experienced success or heard about others' success stories.

For example, an entrepreneur who has just witnessed a competitor fail may become overly cautious, avoiding risks that are necessary for their own growth. On the other hand, someone who has recently had a string of successful investments may become overly optimistic, ignoring warning signs that suggest a downturn.

The key to countering the availability heuristic is to rely on objective data rather than personal anecdotes or recent experiences. Just because a particular outcome is fresh in your mind doesn't mean it's representative of the broader reality. By focusing on facts and probabilities rather than emotionally charged events, you can make more balanced decisions.

3. Confirmation Bias: Seeing What You Want to See

Confirmation bias is the tendency to seek out information that confirms our preexisting beliefs while ignoring or discounting information that contradicts them. In risk-taking, confirmation bias can cause us to focus on data that supports our decision to take a risk while disregarding red flags that suggest caution.

For example, if you're excited about starting a new business, you may selectively focus on success stories of entrepreneurs who have thrived in similar industries while dismissing statistics about the high failure rate of startups. This bias can lead to overly optimistic assessments of risk and an underestimation of potential challenges.

To overcome confirmation bias, it's important to actively seek out information that challenges your assumptions. Make a conscious effort to consider opposing viewpoints and assess the full spectrum of data before making a decision. By doing so, you'll gain a more comprehensive understanding of the risks involved and be better equipped to make informed choices.

Managing Emotions and Biases in Risk-Taking

Given the powerful influence of emotions and cognitive biases on risk-taking, how can we ensure that our decisions are grounded in rationality rather than impulsiveness? The key lies in developing self-awareness and implementing strategies to manage these psychological factors.

First, it's important to cultivate emotional intelligence—the ability to recognize, understand, and manage your own emotions. By becoming more aware of how emotions like fear, excitement, and overconfidence affect your decision-making, you can take steps to mitigate their influence. This might involve pausing before making a decision, seeking input from trusted advisors, or using tools like journaling to clarify your thoughts and feelings.

Second, practicing mindfulness can help you stay present and focused when faced with risky decisions. Mindfulness involves paying attention to the present moment without judgment, which can help you avoid getting caught up in emotional reactions or cognitive biases. By staying grounded and centered, you'll be better able to evaluate risks objectively.

Finally, using structured decision-making processes can help counteract the impact of biases. This might involve creating a checklist of factors to consider before taking a risk, conducting a thorough risk-reward analysis, or using decision matrices to weigh different options. By introducing structure and logic into your decision-making, you can reduce the influence of emotions and biases and make more informed, balanced choices.

Chapter 4: CALCULATED RISK VS. RECKLESS RISK

In life and business, taking risks is unavoidable. Whether it's making a bold career move, investing in a new venture, or taking on a significant personal challenge, risk plays an integral role in growth and progress. However, not all risks are created equal. The key to success lies in distinguishing between calculated risks—those taken with a clear understanding of potential outcomes and a plan for mitigating loss—and reckless risks, which are driven by impulsivity and often lead to unnecessary failures.

Understanding the difference between calculated risk and reckless risk is critical for making sound decisions that lead to success rather than catastrophe. While both types of risk involve uncertainty, the approach, mindset, and level of preparedness involved in each are dramatically different. This chapter goes deep into the nature of these two forms of risk, helping you identify when you're making a smart, calculated move and when you might be venturing into reckless territory.

The Anatomy of Calculated Risk

Calculated risk involves taking action after careful evaluation of the potential outcomes, understanding the consequences, and putting strategies in place to maximize rewards while minimizing loss. People who take calculated risks don't shy away from uncertainty, but they approach it methodically, gathering as much information as possible, analyzing the data, and weighing the potential gains against the potential losses.

At its core, calculated risk is about control. You can't eliminate uncertainty entirely, but you can significantly reduce the element of surprise by being prepared and informed. Calculated risk-takers are often seen as strategic thinkers who use logic and reason to guide their decisions.

So, what does calculated risk entail?

1. Research and Information Gathering

Before taking a calculated risk, successful individuals invest significant time and effort into researching the situation. This might include analyzing market conditions, studying trends, gathering feedback from experienced professionals, or examining similar situations from the past. The more information you have, the better equipped you are to make a decision that maximizes your chances of success. For example, an entrepreneur considering launching a new product will conduct thorough market research, study the competition, and assess customer demand before investing capital.

2. Understanding the Risk-Reward Ratio

Calculated risk-takers evaluate the risk-reward ratio of a potential action. This is a key component of deciding whether a risk is worth taking. The risk-reward ratio is the comparison between the potential downside of a risk (losses) and the potential upside (gains). A smart risk-taker won't shy away from risks, but they will only take risks when the potential rewards significantly outweigh the possible losses. If the risk of failure is too high or the reward isn't substantial enough, it's a clear signal to reconsider the action.

For example, if you are considering making a financial investment in a volatile stock, a calculated risk would involve assessing the potential profit you could make if the stock performs well versus the amount of money you could lose if the stock crashes. You would also evaluate your ability to absorb the loss without significant harm to your financial stability.

3. Planning and Risk Mitigation

Calculated risks involve developing a well-thought-out plan and anticipating challenges or setbacks. Successful individuals have a contingency plan in place, which means they are prepared to adjust their approach if things go wrong. This involves identifying possible pitfalls, considering worst-case scenarios, and determining how to mitigate or minimize damage if the risk doesn't pay off. In other words, calculated risk-takers always have an exit strategy or backup plan.

For example, a business owner launching a new product will consider different sales channels, budget for marketing, anticipate potential production delays, and have a backup source of funding in case sales don't meet expectations.

4. Managing Emotions

One of the key differences between calculated and reckless risks lies in emotional control. Calculated risk-takers make decisions based on facts, data, and logical reasoning. They are aware of their emotional responses, such as fear or excitement, but they don't let those emotions cloud their judgment. They have the discipline to pause, reflect, and analyze before acting. This emotional control prevents impulsive decisions and helps them stay calm under pressure.

For example, someone considering a major career change might feel a rush of excitement at the prospect of a new opportunity but will resist the temptation to act immediately. Instead, they will carefully consider the pros and cons, assess their financial situation, and map out a plan before making the leap.

The Dangers of Reckless Risk

Reckless risk, on the other hand, is the opposite of calculated risk. It is characterized by impulsivity, poor planning, and a lack of foresight. People who take reckless risks act without fully understanding the potential consequences, often driven by emotion rather than reason. This can lead to devastating outcomes, including financial ruin, damaged relationships, or missed opportunities for growth.

Reckless risk-takers tend to focus more on the immediate thrill or potential reward without taking the time to evaluate the downsides. They often underestimate the challenges and overestimate their ability to handle setbacks.

So, what are the warning signs of reckless risk?

1. Lack of Research and Preparation

Reckless risk-takers typically jump into a decision without gathering enough information. They may rely on gut instinct, hearsay, or incomplete data, leading them to make uninformed choices. This approach is especially dangerous in areas like business or investing, where understanding the landscape and market conditions is crucial to success. Failing to do adequate research increases the likelihood of failure because the decision-maker is flying blind.

For example, an investor might hear a tip about a hot new stock and immediately pour money into it without checking the company's financial health, market position, or potential risks. This impulsive move can lead to significant losses if the stock underperforms or if the market turns against it.

2. Overconfidence and Ignoring Risks

Reckless risk-takers often exhibit overconfidence, assuming they are immune to failure or that the odds are in their favor without fully considering the risks. This overconfidence can stem from past successes or simply from an inflated sense of their abilities. Overconfident individuals tend to downplay the potential downsides and fail to anticipate worst-case scenarios.

For instance, an entrepreneur who has experienced early success may become overly optimistic and start expanding their business rapidly without evaluating market conditions or securing enough capital. Their overconfidence can lead to overextension, financial strain, and eventual failure.

3. Emotional Decision-Making

Reckless risks are often driven by emotions—whether it's the thrill of a new opportunity, the fear of missing out, or the desire for immediate gratification. When emotions take the wheel, rational thinking takes a backseat. Emotional decision-making is impulsive, reactive, and often results in poor outcomes because it lacks careful thought and planning.

For example, someone may decide to quit their job on a whim after having a bad day, without having another job lined up or a financial safety net in place. This reckless decision, driven by frustration or anger, can lead to long-term financial insecurity and regret.

4. Ignoring the Risk-Reward Ratio

One of the hallmarks of reckless risk-taking is the disregard for the risk-reward ratio. Reckless individuals either don't bother to calculate the ratio or simply choose to ignore it, focusing solely on the potential reward. This often leads to poor decision-making because they fail to appreciate the magnitude of the possible losses.

For example, someone might decide to start a business based solely on the allure of potential profits, without considering the financial risk, the time commitment, or the potential for failure. They may ignore warning signs, such as insufficient market demand or fierce competition, which ultimately leads to the business's collapse.

Identifying the Line Between Calculated and Reckless Risk

The line between calculated and reckless risk can sometimes be subtle, but learning to recognize the difference is essential for making sound decisions. Here are a few key questions to ask yourself when evaluating a risk:

1. Do you have enough information to make an informed decision?

If you haven't taken the time to research and gather all the relevant data, you may be venturing into reckless territory. Calculated risk requires a solid foundation of knowledge and understanding.

2. Have you evaluated the risk-reward ratio?

If you're focusing solely on the potential reward without considering the downside, you're likely taking a reckless risk. A calculated risk involves weighing the potential gains against the potential losses and determining whether the reward justifies the risk.

3. Do you have a plan in place?

If you're jumping into a decision without a clear plan or strategy, you're likely acting recklessly. Calculated risks involve preparation, planning, and risk mitigation strategies to minimize potential losses.

4. Are your emotions driving the decision?

If your decision is driven primarily by excitement, fear, or impatience, it's time to pause and reevaluate. Calculated risk-takers manage their emotions and make decisions based on logic and reason rather than impulsive feelings.

5. What's the worst that could happen?

If you haven't considered the worst-case scenario and how you would handle it, you're probably taking a reckless risk. Calculated risk involves anticipating potential challenges and preparing for setbacks.

Balancing Risk and Reward for Long-Term Success

Ultimately, success in any venture—whether personal, professional, or financial—depends on your ability to balance risk and reward. Calculated risks allow you to seize opportunities for growth while minimizing potential losses. On the other hand, reckless risks may bring short-term excitement but often lead to long-term failure.

Mastering the art of calculated risk-taking requires a combination of self-awareness, emotional control, and strategic thinking. It's about recognizing when a risk is worth taking and when it's better to walk away. By developing these skills, you can make informed decisions that lead to greater success and satisfaction, both in your personal life and your career.

Chapter 5: THE ROLE OF UNCERTAINTY

Uncertainty is an intrinsic part of risk, and it influences every decision we make. Whether you're venturing into a new business, investing in the stock market, or making a personal decision that could affect your future, uncertainty is always present.

Uncertainty refers to the lack of complete certainty or predictability regarding future events. It manifests in various forms and affects different aspects of life and decision-making processes. In essence, uncertainty involves not knowing what will happen next, despite having some information or data.

Types of Uncertainty

Uncertainty can be categorized into several types:

- Ambiguity: This type of uncertainty arises from unclear or incomplete information. When the future is ambiguous, it's difficult to predict outcomes because the available data is insufficient or unreliable. For example, a startup business entering a new market may face ambiguity about consumer preferences and competitive dynamics.

- Volatility: This form of uncertainty involves the rapid and unpredictable changes in variables. In financial markets, volatility refers to the fluctuations in asset prices that make forecasting difficult. High volatility can lead to significant changes in market conditions, affecting investment strategies.
- Complexity: Complexity arises when multiple interconnected factors influence an outcome. In complex systems, such as global supply chains or large organizations, the interplay of various components creates uncertainty. Understanding how changes in one part of the system impact others can be challenging.
- Ambiguity Aversion: Some individuals prefer certainty and may avoid situations with ambiguous outcomes, even if the potential rewards are high. This aversion to ambiguity can lead to missed opportunities and conservative decision-making.

The Impact of Uncertainty on Decision-Making

Uncertainty affects decision-making in profound ways. It introduces a range of emotions and cognitive processes that influence how we approach risks and make choices.

- Fear and Anxiety: Uncertainty often triggers fear and anxiety. When faced with the unknown, people may worry about potential negative outcomes and the lack of control over future events. This fear can lead to hesitation or avoidance of risky decisions.
- Cognitive Biases: Cognitive biases, such as overconfidence or loss aversion, can distort our perception of uncertainty. Overconfidence might lead individuals to underestimate risks, while loss aversion can make them overly cautious. These biases can impact decision-making by skewing our assessment of potential outcomes.
- Decision Paralysis: High levels of uncertainty can lead to decision paralysis, where individuals are unable to make a choice due to fear of making the wrong decision. This paralysis can result in missed opportunities and stagnation.

Embracing Uncertainty: Turning Challenges into Opportunities

While uncertainty can be daunting, it also presents opportunities for growth and innovation. Embracing uncertainty involves shifting your mindset from fear to curiosity and leveraging the unknown to your advantage.

1. Adopting a Growth Mindset

A growth mindset is essential for embracing uncertainty. Individuals with a growth mindset view challenges as opportunities for learning and development. They are more likely to take calculated risks, adapt to changing circumstances, and persist in the face of setbacks. This mindset encourages exploration and experimentation, leading to new insights and possibilities.

For example, an entrepreneur entering an emerging industry might face uncertainty about market demand and competition. By adopting a growth mindset, they can view this uncertainty as an opportunity to innovate, experiment with different approaches, and learn from their experiences.

2. Building Resilience

Resilience is the ability to bounce back from adversity and adapt to changing conditions. Developing resilience helps individuals manage uncertainty more effectively and remain focused on their goals despite setbacks. Resilient individuals view challenges as temporary and surmountable, allowing them to persevere and maintain a positive outlook.

Strategies for building resilience include:

- Developing Coping Skills: Effective coping strategies, such as mindfulness, stress management, and problem-solving skills, can help individuals navigate uncertainty and maintain emotional stability.
- Setting Realistic Goals: Setting realistic and achievable goals provides a sense of direction and purpose, helping individuals stay motivated and focused during uncertain times.
- Learning from Failure: Embracing failure as a learning opportunity rather than a defeat fosters resilience. Analyzing failures, identifying lessons learned, and applying those lessons to future endeavors can strengthen resilience.

3. Embracing Flexibility and Adaptability

Flexibility and adaptability are crucial for navigating uncertainty. In a rapidly changing environment, the ability to adjust plans and strategies based on new information or shifting conditions is essential for success. Flexibility allows individuals to pivot when necessary and seize emerging opportunities.

For example, a business operating in a volatile market may need to adapt its strategies frequently based on market trends, consumer preferences, or regulatory changes. Being flexible and open to change enables the business to remain competitive and capitalize on new opportunities.

4. Leveraging Uncertainty for Innovation

Uncertainty can be a catalyst for innovation. When the future is uncertain, individuals and organizations are often prompted to think creatively and explore novel solutions. Uncertainty encourages experimentation and risk-taking, leading to breakthroughs and advancements.

For instance, in the technology sector, uncertainty about future trends and consumer needs drives companies to innovate and develop new products. Companies that embrace uncertainty are more likely to pioneer new technologies and disrupt existing markets.

5. Developing Strategic Scenarios

Strategic scenario planning involves creating multiple scenarios for different possible futures and developing strategies for each scenario. This approach helps individuals and organizations prepare for various outcomes and make informed decisions despite uncertainty.

Scenario planning involves:

- Identifying Key Uncertainties: Determine the factors that could impact future outcomes and create scenarios based on different possible developments.
- Developing Action Plans: Create strategies and action plans for each scenario, outlining how to respond to various outcomes and manage potential risks.
- Monitoring and Adjusting: Continuously monitor changes in the environment and adjust strategies as needed based on new information or developments.

Practical Applications of Embracing Uncertainty

Embracing uncertainty can lead to practical benefits and improvements in various areas of life and business. Here are some practical applications:

1. Career Development

In career development, uncertainty about future opportunities and job markets can drive individuals to acquire new skills, pursue further education, or explore different career paths. Embracing uncertainty allows individuals to adapt to changing job markets and position themselves for future success.

2. Investment Strategies

In investing, uncertainty about market conditions and economic trends encourages diversification and risk management strategies. Investors who embrace uncertainty are more likely to explore various investment options, balance their portfolios, and make informed decisions based on changing market dynamics.

3. Business Strategy

Businesses operating in uncertain environments can benefit from adopting flexible strategies and fostering a culture of innovation. Embracing uncertainty enables businesses to respond to changing consumer demands, adapt to new technologies, and identify emerging market opportunities.

4. Personal Growth

On a personal level, embracing uncertainty can lead to growth and self-discovery. Taking risks, exploring new experiences, and stepping out of comfort zones can lead to personal development, increased confidence, and a greater sense of fulfillment.

Chapter 6: RISK IN BUSINESS AND ENTREPRENEURSHIP

Risk is an inherent component of business and entrepreneurship, driving both innovation and growth. This chapter explores how business leaders and entrepreneurs manage risk to navigate uncertainties and seize opportunities. Through examining various strategies and real-world examples, we can understand how calculated risk-taking contributes to success and how to effectively mitigate potential downsides.

The Role of Risk in Business and Entrepreneurship

In the world of business, risk is not merely an obstacle to be avoided but a vital element that can lead to significant rewards. Entrepreneurs and business leaders often face uncertain conditions, including market fluctuations, competitive pressures, and technological changes. Embracing and managing these risks is crucial for fostering innovation, driving growth, and achieving long-term success.

1. The Nature of Business Risk

Business risk encompasses a range of uncertainties that can impact an organization's performance. These risks can be classified into several categories:

- Market Risk: This type of risk arises from changes in market conditions, such as shifts in consumer preferences, economic downturns, or new competitors entering the market. Market risk affects demand for products or services and can influence pricing strategies and sales forecasts.
- Operational Risk: Operational risk involves uncertainties related to the internal processes and systems of a business. This includes risks associated with supply chain disruptions, production inefficiencies, technology failures, and human resources issues.
- Financial Risk: Financial risk pertains to the management of financial resources, including risks related to cash flow, debt, and investment decisions. Businesses must balance their financial strategies to ensure liquidity and profitability while managing exposure to interest rate changes, currency fluctuations, and credit risks.
- Strategic Risk: Strategic risk arises from the decisions and actions taken by a company's leadership. This

includes risks associated with strategic initiatives, such as entering new markets, launching new products, or pursuing mergers and acquisitions. Strategic risk is closely tied to the long-term vision and goals of the organization.

2. Embracing Risk for Innovation

Innovation often requires stepping into the unknown and taking calculated risks. Business leaders who embrace risk are more likely to pioneer new ideas, explore novel approaches, and differentiate themselves in the market. Risk-taking can lead to groundbreaking products, services, and business models that drive competitive advantage and growth.

3. Balancing Risk and Reward

Effective risk management involves striking a balance between risk and reward. Business leaders must assess potential risks against the expected rewards to make informed decisions. This involves evaluating the likelihood of success, potential returns, and the impact of potential setbacks.

Strategies for Managing Risk in Business

To successfully manage risk, entrepreneurs and business leaders employ various strategies. These strategies aim to mitigate potential downsides while capitalizing on opportunities.

1. Risk Assessment and Analysis

Risk assessment involves identifying and evaluating potential risks that could affect a business. This process includes:

- Risk Identification: Recognizing potential risks that could impact the organization. This involves analyzing internal and external factors, such as market trends, operational challenges, and regulatory changes.
- Risk Analysis: Evaluating the likelihood and impact of identified risks. Risk analysis helps prioritize risks based on their potential severity and the organization's ability to mitigate them.
- Risk Evaluation: Comparing the results of risk analysis with the organization's risk tolerance and objectives. This evaluation helps determine the appropriate risk management strategies.

2. Diversification

Diversification is a key strategy for managing risk by spreading investments or resources across different areas. This can involve:

- Product Diversification: Offering a range of products or services to reduce dependence on a single revenue stream. For example, a technology company might diversify its product line to include software, hardware, and services.
- Market Diversification: Expanding into new markets or regions to reduce exposure to economic fluctuations in a single market. For instance, a company operating in multiple countries can mitigate risks associated with regional economic downturns.
- Investment Diversification: Allocating investments across various asset classes or financial instruments to reduce exposure to market volatility. Diversification helps manage financial risk and achieve more stable returns.

3. Risk Mitigation and Contingency Planning

Risk mitigation involves implementing strategies to minimize the impact of potential risks. This includes:

- Developing Contingency Plans: Creating plans to address potential risks and disruptions. Contingency plans outline steps to be taken in response to specific scenarios, such as supply chain disruptions, technology failures, or natural disasters.
- Implementing Risk Controls: Establishing processes and controls to prevent or minimize risks. This includes measures such as quality control, security protocols, and compliance checks.
- Monitoring and Reviewing Risks: Continuously monitoring risk factors and reviewing risk management strategies. Regular reviews help identify emerging risks and assess the effectiveness of existing controls.

Case Studies: Successful Risk Management

Examining real-world examples of companies that have successfully managed risk can provide valuable insights into effective risk management strategies.

1. Apple Inc.

Apple Inc. is a prime example of a company that has effectively managed risk while driving innovation. The company's risk management strategy includes:

- Product Diversification: Apple has diversified its product portfolio to include a range of devices, such as iPhones, iPads, Macs, and wearables. This diversification reduces reliance on any single product and helps mitigate market risks.

- Market Expansion: Apple has expanded its presence in global markets, allowing it to tap into new customer bases and reduce exposure to regional economic fluctuations.

- Innovation and R&D: Apple invests heavily in research and development to drive innovation and maintain a competitive edge. The company's focus on developing new technologies and products helps it stay ahead of competitors and adapt to changing market conditions.

2. Tesla Inc.

Tesla Inc. exemplifies how risk-taking can lead to groundbreaking innovation. The company's approach to managing risk includes:

- Technology Development: Tesla has invested in developing advanced technologies for electric vehicles and renewable energy. This focus on innovation has positioned Tesla as a leader in the clean energy sector and has driven significant growth.

- Vertical Integration: Tesla's vertical integration strategy involves controlling multiple stages of the supply chain, from manufacturing to distribution. This approach helps mitigate supply chain risks and improve efficiency.

- Strategic Partnerships: Tesla has formed strategic partnerships with other companies and organizations to advance its goals. Collaborations with battery manufacturers, technology providers, and governments help Tesla manage risks and achieve its objectives.

3. Amazon.com

Amazon.com provides an example of how risk management and diversification contribute to business success. The company's risk management strategies include:

- E-Commerce Expansion: Amazon has diversified its business model beyond e-commerce to include cloud computing (AWS), digital media, and logistics. This diversification reduces reliance on any single revenue stream and helps mitigate market risks.

- Global Operations: Amazon operates in multiple countries and regions, allowing it to reach a broad customer base and reduce exposure to regional economic fluctuations.

- Technology Investments: Amazon invests in technology and innovation to improve its operations and enhance customer experiences. The company's focus on automation, artificial intelligence, and data analytics helps it stay competitive and adapt to changing market conditions.

Risk is an integral part of business and entrepreneurship, driving innovation, growth, and competitive advantage. By understanding and managing risk effectively, entrepreneurs and business leaders can navigate uncertainties, capitalize on opportunities, and achieve long-term success.

Successful risk management involves assessing potential risks, implementing mitigation strategies, and embracing opportunities for growth and innovation. Real-world examples of companies that have effectively managed risk provide valuable insights into how calculated risk-taking can lead to significant rewards.

As businesses continue to operate in dynamic and uncertain environments, the ability to manage risk strategically will remain a key factor in achieving success and sustaining growth. Embracing risk as a catalyst for innovation and leveraging effective risk management strategies can help organizations thrive in an ever-changing world.

Chapter 7: FINANCIAL RISK AND REWARD

Financial risk refers to the potential for loss or lower-than-expected returns associated with investment decisions. It arises from the uncertainty of financial markets and economic conditions, and can manifest in various forms:

- Market Risk: The risk of losses due to fluctuations in market prices, including stock prices, interest rates, and commodity prices. Market risk is inherent in all investments and can be influenced by economic events, geopolitical developments, and changes in investor sentiment.
- Credit Risk: The risk that a borrower will default on their debt obligations, leading to a loss for the lender or investor. Credit risk is particularly relevant for fixed-income investments, such as bonds and loans.
- Liquidity Risk: The risk of being unable to sell an investment quickly at its fair market value due to a lack of buyers or market depth. Liquidity risk can affect investments in less liquid markets or assets.

- Interest Rate Risk: The risk that changes in interest rates will negatively impact the value of investments. For example, rising interest rates can lead to a decline in bond prices, while falling rates can reduce the returns on interest-bearing investments.
- Inflation Risk: The risk that inflation will erode the purchasing power of investment returns. Inflation risk is a concern for long-term investments, as rising prices can reduce the real value of future cash flows.

The Concept of Reward

Reward, in the financial context, refers to the potential returns or benefits gained from taking on risk. The reward is typically measured in terms of financial gains, such as:

- Capital Gains: The profit earned from selling an investment at a higher price than its purchase price. Capital gains are a common source of reward for investors in stocks, real estate, and other assets.
- Dividend Income: The payments made to shareholders from a company's profits. Dividends provide a steady stream of income and can be a key component of total returns for stock investors.

- Interest Income: The returns earned from interest-bearing investments, such as bonds, savings accounts, and certificates of deposit. Interest income provides regular cash flow and can contribute to overall investment returns.
- Yield: The income generated from an investment relative to its cost or market value. Yield can be expressed as a percentage and is commonly used to evaluate the attractiveness of income-generating investments.

Risk-Reward Trade-Off

The risk-reward trade-off is a fundamental concept in finance that illustrates the relationship between the level of risk and the potential for reward. Generally, higher levels of risk are associated with the possibility of higher returns, while lower levels of risk tend to offer more stable but lower returns. Understanding this trade-off is essential for making investment decisions and constructing a balanced portfolio.

1. High-Risk, High-Reward Investments

High-risk investments offer the potential for significant rewards but come with increased uncertainty and the possibility of substantial losses. Examples of high-risk investments include:

- Stocks: Investing in individual stocks can yield high returns, especially if the company experiences significant growth. However, stock prices can be volatile, and there is a risk of losing the entire investment if the company performs poorly.
- Startups and Venture Capital: Investing in early-stage companies or startups can lead to substantial returns if the business succeeds. However, these investments carry a high level of risk, as many startups fail to achieve profitability or growth.
- Cryptocurrencies: Digital currencies like Bitcoin and Ethereum have experienced dramatic price swings and offer the potential for substantial gains. However, the cryptocurrency market is highly speculative and subject to regulatory uncertainties.

2. Low-Risk, Low-Reward Investments

Low-risk investments typically provide more stable returns but may offer lower potential rewards. Examples of low-risk investments include:

- Government Bonds: Bonds issued by governments, such as U.S. Treasury bonds, are considered low-risk investments because they are backed by the government's credit. However, the returns on government bonds are generally lower compared to stocks or corporate bonds.
- Savings Accounts: Savings accounts offer a safe place to park money with minimal risk. While the returns are low, they provide liquidity and security for short-term savings.
- Certificates of Deposit (CDs): CDs are time deposits offered by banks with fixed interest rates and maturities. They are low-risk investments but typically offer lower returns compared to other investment options.

Investment Strategies and Risk Management

Successful investing requires a careful balance between risk and reward. Investors use various strategies to manage risk and optimize returns, including:

1. Diversification

Diversification involves spreading investments across different asset classes, sectors, and geographic regions to reduce exposure to any single risk. By diversifying a portfolio, investors can mitigate the impact of adverse events on individual investments and achieve more stable overall returns.

2. Asset Allocation

Asset allocation refers to the distribution of investments among different asset classes, such as stocks, bonds, and real estate. A well-designed asset allocation strategy aligns with an investor's risk tolerance, time horizon, and financial goals. It helps manage risk by ensuring that the portfolio is not overly concentrated in one asset class.

3. Risk Assessment and Due Diligence

Before making investment decisions, investors conduct risk assessments and due diligence to evaluate the potential risks and rewards of an investment. This involves analyzing financial statements, assessing market conditions, and considering the investment's historical performance and future prospects.

4. Hedging

Hedging involves using financial instruments or strategies to offset potential losses from adverse market movements.

Common hedging techniques include options, futures contracts, and diversification. Hedging can help protect investments from unexpected changes in market conditions.

5. Monitoring and Rebalancing

Regular monitoring and rebalancing of a portfolio are essential for managing risk and ensuring that the asset allocation remains aligned with the investor's objectives. Rebalancing involves adjusting the portfolio to maintain the desired risk-return profile and respond to changes in market conditions.

Case Studies: Financial Risk and Reward in Action

Examining real-world examples of financial risk and reward can provide valuable insights into how risk management strategies are applied in practice:

1. The Dot-Com Bubble

The dot-com bubble of the late 1990s and early 2000s provides an example of high-risk, high-reward investing. Many investors poured money into technology stocks, driven by the excitement of the internet revolution. While some investors achieved significant gains, the bubble burst in

2000, leading to substantial losses for those who had invested heavily in overvalued technology companies.

2. The Global Financial Crisis of 2008

The global financial crisis of 2008 demonstrated the impact of financial risk on the broader economy. The crisis was triggered by the collapse of the subprime mortgage market and led to widespread losses in financial markets. Investors who had taken on excessive risk in mortgage-backed securities and other high-risk assets faced severe losses, while those who had diversified and managed risk effectively were better positioned to weather the storm.

3. The Rise of Exchange-Traded Funds (ETFs)

Exchange-traded funds (ETFs) have become a popular investment vehicle due to their diversification benefits and cost-effectiveness. ETFs allow investors to gain exposure to a broad range of assets, such as stocks, bonds, and commodities, with lower fees compared to traditional mutual funds. The growth of ETFs reflects the importance of diversification and risk management in achieving long-term investment success.

Chapter 8: RISK AND PERSONAL GROWTH

Risk is often seen as a threat, a hurdle to be avoided in the quest for stability and comfort. Yet, a closer look reveals that risk, when approached thoughtfully, is a powerful driver of personal growth and self-discovery. This chapter delves into the transformative role of risk, the benefits of stepping out of your comfort zone, and how embracing the possibility of failure can pave the way to long-term success.

The Role of Risk in Personal Growth

1. Defining Personal Growth

Personal growth is the ongoing process of improving oneself by developing skills, enhancing self-awareness, and building emotional resilience. It involves stepping beyond the boundaries of one's current capabilities and challenging preconceived limitations. Key elements include:

- **Self-Awareness:** Recognizing and understanding your values, strengths, and areas for improvement.

- **Skill Development:** Learning new skills to achieve personal and professional milestones.
- **Emotional Resilience:** Strengthening your ability to face challenges with a constructive mindset.

Risk serves as a catalyst in this journey, compelling individuals to confront fears, surmount barriers, and unlock potential.

2. Escaping the Comfort Zone

The comfort zone is a psychological space where familiarity and predictability provide a sense of security. While it offers stability, staying confined to this zone can hinder growth. Escaping it requires:

- **Pursuing New Challenges:** Engaging in activities that stretch your capabilities, such as acquiring new skills or taking on leadership roles.
- **Embracing Uncertainty:** Acknowledging that growth often comes with discomfort and unpredictability.
- **Broadening Perspectives:** Seeking diverse experiences to uncover hidden talents and passions.

By deliberately stepping beyond the comfort zone, you can embrace a world of transformative opportunities.

The Benefits of Embracing Risk

1. Enhancing Confidence and Self-Efficacy

Overcoming challenges and taking risks builds belief in your abilities. Success in uncertain situations fosters:

- **Confidence:** Strengthening trust in your decision-making and problem-solving skills.
- **Resilience:** Learning to recover from setbacks equips you to face future challenges.
- **A Growth Mindset:** Viewing obstacles as opportunities for improvement rather than threats.

2. Cultivating Creativity and Innovation

Risk-taking often involves exploring uncharted paths, fostering:

- **Creative Problem-Solving:** Developing unconventional solutions when traditional approaches fail.

- **Discovering New Opportunities:** Unveiling fresh ideas and innovative strategies that drive personal and professional breakthroughs.

3. Strengthening Leadership Abilities

Effective leaders are characterized by their willingness to take calculated risks. Risk-taking hones essential leadership skills, such as:

- **Strategic Decision-Making:** Weighing risks and rewards to make informed choices.
- **Visionary Thinking:** Identifying and pursuing long-term opportunities.
- **Inspiration:** Leading by example and motivating others through courageous actions.

Managing Risk for Optimal Growth

1. Risk Assessment and Evaluation

To maximize growth, risks should be approached methodically:

- **Identify Challenges:** Analyze potential obstacles and uncertainties.
- **Weigh Benefits:** Balance the rewards of growth against the likelihood of setbacks.
- **Prepare Contingencies:** Develop plans to address possible difficulties and minimize negative outcomes.

2. Embracing Failure as a Teacher

Failure, often viewed negatively, is a natural and valuable part of taking risks. To leverage failure for growth:

- **Learn from Mistakes:** Reflect on failures to extract actionable lessons.
- **Build Resilience:** Strengthen your ability to recover and adapt.
- **Adopt Positivity:** See failure as a step forward rather than a permanent barrier.

3. Seeking Guidance and Feedback

The journey of risk-taking is bolstered by support from others:

- **Cultivate a Support Network:** Surround yourself with mentors and peers who provide encouragement and constructive criticism.
- **Welcome Feedback:** Use insights from others to refine your strategies and enhance decision-making.

Real-Life Examples of Risk Driving Growth

1. Entrepreneurial Success

Entrepreneurs often thrive by taking calculated risks. For instance, Steve Jobs' willingness to challenge norms and embrace uncertainty transformed Apple into a global innovator. His example illustrates the power of risk in achieving groundbreaking success.

2. Career Transitions

Switching careers or industries involves significant risk but can lead to profound growth. Professionals who leave stable jobs to follow their passions often gain fresh perspectives, new skills, and deeper fulfillment.

3. Artistic and Academic Achievements

Creative individuals who push boundaries often achieve extraordinary breakthroughs. Artists experimenting with unconventional techniques or academics pursuing bold hypotheses frequently encounter risk but also uncover unique insights and recognition.

Conclusion

Risk is an essential ingredient in the recipe for personal growth. By embracing uncertainty, venturing beyond your comfort zone, and accepting failure as a stepping stone, you unlock unparalleled opportunities for self-improvement. Thoughtful risk-taking fosters resilience, ignites creativity, and develops leadership skills, laying the foundation for a fulfilling and successful life.

Remember, the path to growth is rarely free of challenges, but with a strategic approach and a support network, you can transform risks into rewards. Embrace risk as a tool for empowerment and personal evolution, and watch as it propels you toward achieving your highest potential.

Chapter 9: MANAGING RISK IN A RELATIONSHIP

Relationships are an integral part of human life, encompassing personal bonds with family, friends, and romantic partners, as well as professional connections with colleagues and business associates. Like financial or business ventures, relationships carry inherent risks. These risks may arise from misunderstandings, conflicts, or mismatched expectations. Effectively managing these risks requires a profound understanding of vulnerability, trust, and communication. This chapter explores these essential components and provides actionable strategies for navigating risks in both personal and professional relationships.

Understanding Risks in Relationships

1. The Nature of Relationship Risks

Relationships are complex and dynamic, often involving intricate emotions, expectations, and interactions. Risks can take various forms, including:

- **Emotional Vulnerability:** Sharing personal thoughts and feelings inherently involves the risk of rejection or judgment. While vulnerability is key to fostering meaningful connections, it must be balanced to avoid emotional harm.
- **Conflicts and Misunderstandings:** Differences in values, communication styles, or expectations can lead to disagreements. If unresolved, these issues can escalate, straining or even damaging relationships.
- **Trust Issues:** Trust is foundational to any relationship, and breaches of trust can result in insecurity and doubt. Rebuilding trust demands time, effort, and consistent behavior.

2. The Role of Vulnerability

Vulnerability is a cornerstone of genuine relationships but requires mindful management:

- **Authenticity:** True connections stem from authenticity, which involves openly sharing strengths,

fears, and weaknesses. While this fosters trust, it also requires the courage to embrace uncertainty.
- **Emotional Sharing:** Expressing emotions and experiences strengthens bonds but carries the risk of misunderstanding or rejection. Choosing the right timing and context is crucial.
- **Resilience:** Developing emotional resilience helps mitigate the negative outcomes of vulnerability. This includes managing rejection and coping with discomfort effectively.

3. Building and Maintaining Trust

Trust, the foundation of any healthy relationship, is cultivated through consistent and transparent actions:

- **Consistency:** Reliability and dependability strengthen trust. Following through on promises is critical.
- **Transparency:** Open communication minimizes misunderstandings, promoting clarity in intentions and expectations.

- **Accountability:** Owning mistakes and demonstrating a commitment to rectifying them helps rebuild trust when it is damaged.

Effective Communication in Relationships

1. The Importance of Communication

Effective communication is the cornerstone of managing relationship risks, as it prevents and resolves conflicts while fostering understanding. Key elements include:

- **Active Listening:** Fully focusing on and understanding the other person's perspective creates a sense of value and mutual respect.
- **Clear Expression:** Articulating thoughts and feelings respectfully prevents misunderstandings. Using "I" statements can help convey emotions without assigning blame.
- **Feedback and Clarification:** Constructive feedback and seeking clarification reduce the likelihood of miscommunications. Asking questions ensures mutual understanding.

2. Handling Conflict Constructively

Conflict is inevitable but can be managed constructively with the right approach:

- **Address Issues Early:** Tackling problems promptly prevents escalation.
- **Stay Calm and Respectful:** A composed demeanor helps maintain productive discussions, avoiding personal attacks.
- **Seek Resolution and Compromise:** Collaborative problem-solving and willingness to compromise foster stronger relationships.

3. Developing Emotional Intelligence

Emotional intelligence enhances relationship management by fostering empathy, self-awareness, and emotional regulation:

- **Self-Awareness:** Recognizing personal emotions and their impact on behavior aids effective communication.
- **Empathy:** Understanding others' emotions and perspectives strengthens connections.

- **Emotional Regulation:** Managing emotional responses constructively helps prevent unnecessary conflicts.

Navigating Risks in Professional Relationships

1. Building Professional Trust

In professional settings, trust is essential for collaboration and success:

- **Delivering Results:** Consistently meeting deadlines and producing quality work builds credibility.
- **Professional Integrity:** Adhering to ethical standards and acting with honesty fosters respect and trust.
- **Respecting Confidentiality:** Handling sensitive information responsibly enhances reputation and trustworthiness.

2. Managing Professional Conflicts

Professional conflicts often stem from differing opinions or goals but can be resolved effectively:

- **Effective Mediation:** Engaging neutral mediators facilitates constructive discussions and resolutions.
- **Solution-Oriented Approach:** Focusing on problem-solving rather than blame encourages collaboration.
- **Maintaining Professionalism:** Respectful interactions ensure that conflicts do not harm professional relationships.

Conclusion

Managing risks in relationships, whether personal or professional, is an ongoing process requiring vulnerability, trust, and effective communication. Embracing vulnerability, fostering trust, and developing emotional intelligence pave the way for meaningful connections. By addressing challenges constructively and committing to continuous improvement, individuals can nurture relationships that thrive on mutual respect, understanding, and collaboration. Through these principles, one can achieve greater fulfillment and success in both personal and professional spheres.

Chapter 10: MITIGATING RISK: STRATEGIES AND TOOLS

In a world characterized by uncertainty and volatility, mitigating risk is essential to protecting oneself and one's assets from the potential negative consequences of risky actions. Whether in personal decision-making, business ventures, or investments, the ability to effectively manage and reduce risk can significantly enhance the likelihood of achieving desired outcomes.

Risk mitigation involves reducing the likelihood or impact of negative outcomes associated with risky actions. Unlike risk avoidance, which seeks to eliminate the risk entirely, mitigation focuses on minimizing potential harm while still pursuing the desired objective. Effective risk mitigation requires identifying potential risks, assessing their potential impact, and implementing strategies to manage or reduce these risks.

The importance of risk mitigation cannot be overstated. It is essential for protecting assets, whether they are financial, physical, or intellectual. By effectively managing risk, individuals and organizations can make informed decisions with a clearer understanding of potential risks and their implications. Furthermore, effective risk mitigation improves resilience, enabling quicker recovery from adverse events and contributing to long-term success and stability.

The Importance of Risk Mitigation

Risk mitigation is crucial for several reasons:

- Protecting Assets: By minimizing potential losses, risk mitigation helps safeguard assets, whether they are financial, physical, or intellectual.
- Enhancing Decision-Making: Effective risk mitigation allows individuals and organizations to make informed decisions with a clearer understanding of potential risks and their implications.
- Improving Resilience: Implementing risk mitigation strategies enhances the ability to withstand and recover from adverse events, contributing to long-term success and stability.

Contingency Planning

What is Contingency Planning?

Contingency planning involves developing a set of predefined actions and responses to address potential risks or adverse events. The goal is to ensure that there is a clear plan in place for managing unexpected situations, thereby minimizing their impact on the overall objectives.

Steps in Developing a Contingency Plan

To create an effective contingency plan, follow these steps:

- Identify Potential Risks: Begin by identifying potential risks that could impact your objectives. This involves assessing internal and external factors that may lead to adverse events. Consider risks such as market fluctuations, operational failures, or natural disasters.
- Assess Impact and Likelihood: Evaluate the potential impact and likelihood of each identified risk. This helps prioritize which risks to address first and determines the level of preparedness required.
- Develop Response Strategies: Create specific response strategies for each identified risk. These strategies should outline the actions to be taken if the risk materializes, including contingency measures, resource allocation, and communication plans.

- Test and Revise: Regularly test the contingency plan through simulations or drills to ensure its effectiveness. Revise the plan as needed based on the results of these tests and any changes in the risk environment.

Benefits of Contingency Planning

Contingency planning offers several benefits:

- Preparedness: Ensures that you are prepared to respond effectively to unexpected events, reducing the impact on your objectives.
- Minimized Disruption: Helps minimize disruption to operations and activities, allowing for a quicker recovery from adverse events.
- Informed Decision-Making: Provides a framework for making informed decisions during crises, enabling more effective and timely responses.

Diversification

Diversification involves spreading investments or resources across various assets, sectors, or activities to reduce the impact of adverse events on the overall portfolio. By diversifying, you reduce the risk of significant losses resulting from the poor performance of a single investment or asset.

Investment diversification involves spreading investments across different asset classes, such as stocks, bonds, real estate, and commodities. This approach reduces the risk associated with the performance of any single asset class. Geographic diversification, on the other hand, involves investing in assets or businesses across different geographic regions. This strategy helps mitigate risks associated with economic downturns or political instability in a specific region. Sector diversification involves investing in different industry sectors to reduce the impact of sector-specific risks. For example, diversifying between technology, healthcare, and consumer goods sectors can buffer against downturns in a particular industry.

The benefits of diversification include risk reduction, stability, and potential for long-term growth. Diversification reduces the overall risk of the portfolio by spreading investments across various assets or sectors. It provides a buffer against volatility and market fluctuations, leading to more stable returns. Additionally, it enhances the potential for long-term growth by capturing opportunities across different areas of the market.

Scenario Analysis

Scenario analysis involves evaluating different possible future scenarios to understand their potential impact on objectives and outcomes. It helps identify how various factors may interact and affect the overall risk profile, enabling better preparedness for uncertain conditions.

To conduct scenario analysis, begin by defining a range of plausible future scenarios, including both optimistic and pessimistic outcomes. These scenarios should reflect different combinations of factors that could impact objectives. Assessing the potential impact of each scenario involves analyzing how these scenarios might affect key variables such as financial performance, operational efficiency, or market conditions.

Developing response plans for each scenario involves outlining actions to be taken under different conditions. These plans should address potential challenges and opportunities presented by each scenario. Regularly monitoring changes in the risk environment and updating scenarios and response plans accordingly ensures that preparedness remains relevant and effective.

Scenario analysis offers several benefits, including enhanced preparedness, informed decision-making, and strategic planning. It provides a framework for preparing for a range of possible future conditions, improving resilience and adaptability. Additionally, it supports strategic planning by identifying opportunities and challenges under various scenarios, facilitating more effective long-term planning.

Implementing Risk Mitigation Strategies

To effectively implement risk mitigation strategies, integrate them into the decision-making process. This involves considering risk mitigation as part of the planning and evaluation stages for any project or investment. Ensure that all relevant stakeholders are involved in the risk assessment and mitigation process.

Regular monitoring and evaluation are essential for assessing the effectiveness of risk mitigation strategies. Track key risk indicators, assess the impact of implemented strategies, and make necessary adjustments based on changing conditions. Adopting a continuous improvement approach to risk management involves regularly reviewing and updating risk mitigation strategies, incorporating lessons learned from past experiences, and adapting to new risks and opportunities.

Chapter 11: THE COST OF AVOIDING RISK

Risk is an inherent aspect of life and business, shaping decisions, opportunities, and growth. While risk management is crucial for mitigating potential negative outcomes, avoiding risk altogether can lead to significant drawbacks. This chapter examines the dangers of completely steering clear of risk, exploring how excessive caution can result in stagnation, missed opportunities, and reduced potential for both personal and professional advancement.

The Nature of Risk Aversion

Risk aversion is a psychological and behavioral tendency to avoid actions or decisions that could lead to negative outcomes. This inclination is driven by a natural desire to protect oneself from harm and preserve stability. While risk aversion can be beneficial in situations requiring caution, such as health or safety-related decisions, it can become detrimental when applied indiscriminately to all aspects of life and business.

When individuals or organizations become excessively risk-averse, they often prioritize avoiding losses over pursuing potential gains. This mindset can lead to an aversion to new experiences, opportunities, and innovations. Risk aversion is influenced by several factors, including past experiences, psychological biases, and societal norms. For example, individuals who have experienced significant losses in the past may develop a heightened fear of risk, leading them to avoid similar situations in the future.

The Perils of Playing It Too Safe

1. Stagnation and Lack of Growth

One of the most significant costs of avoiding risk is stagnation. When individuals or businesses consistently avoid risk, they limit their potential for growth and progress. Growth often requires stepping out of one's comfort zone and embracing new challenges. By avoiding risk, individuals and organizations miss opportunities to innovate, explore new markets, and develop new skills.

In business, a risk-averse approach can lead to a lack of innovation and competitiveness. Companies that avoid taking calculated risks may fail to adapt to changing market conditions, falling behind competitors who are willing to experiment and innovate. This stagnation can result in decreased market share, reduced profitability, and ultimately, business failure.

Similarly, in personal life, excessive risk aversion can hinder personal development and fulfillment. Individuals who avoid taking risks may miss out on opportunities for career advancement, personal growth, and meaningful experiences. This can lead to a sense of unfulfilled potential and dissatisfaction.

2. Missed Opportunities

Avoiding risk often means missing out on valuable opportunities. Many of life's most rewarding experiences and achievements involve some degree of risk. Whether it's pursuing a new career path, starting a business, or investing in a new venture, these opportunities come with inherent risks but also the potential for significant rewards.

In business, opportunities for growth and success often involve risk. For example, launching a new product or entering a new market requires investing resources and facing uncertainty. Companies that avoid these opportunities due to fear of risk may miss out on potential revenue streams, market share, and competitive advantages.

On a personal level, avoiding risk can mean missing out on life-changing experiences. Taking risks, such as moving to a new city, starting a new relationship, or pursuing a new hobby, can lead to personal growth and fulfillment. By avoiding these risks, individuals may miss out on opportunities for happiness and personal development.

3. Reduced Adaptability and Resilience

Avoiding risk can also lead to reduced adaptability and resilience. In a rapidly changing world, the ability to adapt to new circumstances and challenges is crucial. Those who avoid risk may become accustomed to a static, predictable environment, which can hinder their ability to respond effectively to change.

In business, adaptability is essential for surviving and thriving in dynamic markets. Companies that avoid risk may struggle to pivot in response to changing customer needs, technological advancements, or competitive pressures. This lack of adaptability can result in missed opportunities and failure to capitalize on emerging trends.

Individually, avoiding risk can lead to a lack of resilience. Facing and overcoming challenges builds strength and adaptability. By avoiding risks, individuals miss opportunities to develop resilience and problem-solving skills, making it more difficult to handle future challenges.

4. Economic and Financial Implications

In the financial realm, avoiding risk can result in missed investment opportunities and reduced financial growth. Many investment opportunities come with risks but also the potential for significant returns. By avoiding these opportunities, individuals and businesses may miss out on potential financial gains.

For example, conservative investment strategies that avoid risk may result in lower returns compared to more aggressive strategies that embrace calculated risks. Similarly, businesses that avoid taking risks may miss out on profitable ventures and growth opportunities.

In personal finance, avoiding risk can lead to missed opportunities for wealth accumulation and financial security. For instance, avoiding investments with higher risks may result in lower returns and slower wealth accumulation over time.

While avoiding risk can have its drawbacks, it is essential to balance risk with reward. The key is not to eliminate risk entirely but to approach it with a strategic mindset. This involves assessing potential risks, evaluating their impact, and making informed decisions based on a thorough understanding of the potential rewards and drawbacks.

Taking calculated risks involves weighing the potential benefits against the possible negative outcomes. This requires careful planning, research, and risk assessment. By adopting a strategic approach to risk, individuals and organizations can pursue opportunities for growth and achievement while minimizing potential downsides.

Strategies for Embracing Risk

1. Assess and Analyze Risks

Before taking any risk, it is crucial to assess and analyze its potential impact. This involves identifying the specific risks involved, evaluating their likelihood, and understanding their potential consequences. Conducting a risk assessment helps in making informed decisions and developing strategies to mitigate potential negative outcomes.

2. Develop a Risk Management Plan

A risk management plan outlines strategies for addressing potential risks and their impact. This plan should include contingency measures, risk mitigation strategies, and response plans. By having a well-defined plan in place, individuals and organizations can navigate risks more effectively and reduce their impact.

3. Embrace a Growth Mindset

Adopting a growth mindset involves viewing challenges and risks as opportunities for learning and development. Embracing this mindset encourages individuals to take risks and pursue new experiences, fostering personal and professional growth. It also helps in building resilience and adaptability.

4. Set Clear Goals and Objectives

Setting clear goals and objectives provides direction and motivation when taking risks. By defining specific goals, individuals and organizations can better assess the potential rewards of taking risks and stay focused on their desired outcomes.

5. Learn from Failures and Successes

Both failures and successes provide valuable insights into risk-taking. Analyzing past experiences helps in understanding what worked and what didn't, allowing for adjustments and improvements in future risk-taking endeavors. Learning from these experiences enhances decision-making and risk management skills.

Avoiding risk altogether can lead to stagnation, missed opportunities, and reduced growth potential. While risk aversion is a natural response to uncertainty, it is essential to balance caution with calculated risk-taking. Assessing risks, developing strategies, and embracing a growth mindset will enable individuals and organizations pursue opportunities for advancement while managing potential negative outcomes.

Taking risks is a fundamental aspect of achieving success and personal fulfillment. By understanding the costs of avoiding risk and adopting a strategic approach to risk management, you can unlock new opportunities, foster growth, and achieve your goals with greater confidence.

Embrace the balance between risk and reward, and you will find that the potential for success often lies just beyond the edge of your comfort zone.

Chapter 12: RISK-TAKING IN LEADERSHIP

Risk-taking is a fundamental aspect of effective leadership, enabling leaders to drive growth, foster innovation, and inspire their teams. This chapter delves into how great leaders balance risk and responsibility, illustrating how they leverage risk as a strategic tool to navigate uncertainty and achieve remarkable results. Through a thorough exploration of leadership dynamics, this chapter provides insights into the delicate art of balancing risk with responsibility, using risk as a catalyst for progress, and guiding others through uncertain terrains.

Understanding the Role of Risk in Leadership

At the heart of effective leadership lies the ability to make decisions under conditions of uncertainty. Risk-taking, when approached with strategic intent, allows leaders to push boundaries, explore new opportunities, and drive their organizations forward. However, the ability to manage risk effectively is crucial for ensuring that the potential rewards outweigh the risks.

Risk-taking in leadership involves more than just making bold decisions. It requires a nuanced understanding of the potential outcomes, the ability to assess risks critically, and the capacity to lead others through the resulting uncertainty. Great leaders embrace risk as an essential component of their strategic toolkit, using it to create value, inspire their teams, and achieve their vision.

The Balance Between Risk and Responsibility

1. Strategic Risk-Taking

Great leaders understand that risk-taking must be strategic rather than reckless. Strategic risk-taking involves evaluating potential risks and rewards, considering the long-term implications of decisions, and aligning risk with organizational goals. Leaders who take strategic risks are more likely to achieve positive outcomes because their decisions are informed by a thorough analysis of potential benefits and drawbacks.

Strategic risk-taking also involves setting clear objectives and defining success metrics. Leaders must ensure that the risks they take are aligned with their organization's vision and mission. By establishing clear goals and measuring success, leaders can better assess the impact of their decisions and make adjustments as needed.

2. Risk as a Catalyst for Innovation

Innovation often requires stepping into the unknown and embracing uncertainty. Leaders who encourage a culture of innovation understand that taking calculated risks can lead to groundbreaking discoveries and advancements. By fostering an environment where experimentation is encouraged, leaders can drive creativity and inspire their teams to explore new possibilities.

Great leaders use risk as a catalyst for innovation by promoting a mindset that values experimentation and learning from failure. They encourage their teams to take risks, challenge the status quo, and pursue novel solutions to problems. This approach not only drives innovation but also builds a resilient organizational culture that can adapt to changing circumstances.

3. Navigating Uncertainty with Confidence

One of the key traits of effective leaders is their ability to navigate uncertainty with confidence. Leaders who manage risk effectively are able to make informed decisions despite the inherent uncertainty of the situation. This confidence is built on a foundation of experience, knowledge, and a clear understanding of the potential risks and rewards.

Leaders who exhibit confidence in the face of uncertainty inspire trust and loyalty among their teams. When leaders demonstrate calmness and decisiveness during challenging times, they reassure their teams and create a sense of stability. This confidence helps teams stay focused and motivated, even when faced with complex and unpredictable situations.

4. Communicating Risk and Responsibility

Effective communication is essential for managing risk and responsibility in leadership. Leaders must be transparent about the risks associated with their decisions, communicate their rationale clearly, and involve their teams in the decision-making process. By fostering open communication, leaders can build trust and ensure that their teams are aligned with the organization's goals.

When communicating about risk, leaders should provide context and explain the reasoning behind their decisions.

This helps team members understand the potential impact of the risks and how they fit into the broader strategy. Clear communication also enables teams to provide feedback, voice concerns, and contribute to the decision-making process.

5. Learning from Failure and Success

Risk-taking inherently involves the possibility of failure. Effective leaders recognize that failure is a natural part of the risk-taking process and view it as an opportunity for learning and growth. By analyzing both successes and failures, leaders can gain valuable insights into what works and what doesn't, allowing them to refine their strategies and make more informed decisions in the future.

Leaders who embrace failure as a learning opportunity foster a culture of resilience and continuous improvement. They encourage their teams to reflect on their experiences, share lessons learned, and apply those insights to future endeavors. This approach not only helps leaders and their teams grow but also strengthens the organization's ability to adapt and thrive.

Case Studies of Risk-Taking Leadership

1. Steve Jobs and Apple

Steve Jobs, co-founder of Apple Inc., is renowned for his risk-taking approach to leadership. Jobs' willingness to take bold risks and challenge conventional thinking played a pivotal role in transforming Apple into one of the most innovative companies in the world. His decision to invest in groundbreaking products like the iPhone and iPad, despite significant uncertainty and potential setbacks, exemplifies strategic risk-taking.

Jobs' leadership was characterized by his ability to envision the future and take calculated risks to bring his vision to life. His approach to innovation and product development was driven by a relentless pursuit of excellence and a willingness to embrace uncertainty. Jobs' legacy demonstrates how effective risk-taking can lead to transformative success and redefine entire industries.

2. Elon Musk and SpaceX

Elon Musk, founder and CEO of SpaceX, is another example of a leader who embraces risk as a catalyst for innovation. Musk's decision to pursue ambitious goals in space exploration, such as reducing the cost of space travel and establishing a human colony on Mars, involved significant risks and challenges. Despite numerous setbacks and technical difficulties, Musk's perseverance and willingness to take risks have led to groundbreaking achievements in space technology.

Musk's leadership style is characterized by his vision, resilience, and willingness to push the boundaries of what is possible. His approach to risk-taking has not only driven technological advancements but also inspired a new generation of innovators and entrepreneurs.

Developing Risk-Taking Leadership Skills

1. Cultivate a Visionary Mindset

Leaders who excel at risk-taking possess a visionary mindset that enables them to see opportunities where others see obstacles. Developing a clear vision for the future and understanding how risk can contribute to achieving that vision is crucial for effective leadership. Leaders should focus on setting ambitious goals and identifying the risks and rewards associated with pursuing their vision.

2. Build Resilience and Adaptability

Resilience and adaptability are essential traits for managing risk effectively. Leaders should work on building their resilience by learning from setbacks, staying focused on their goals, and adapting their strategies as needed. Developing resilience helps leaders navigate uncertainty with confidence and maintain a positive outlook in the face of challenges.

3. Foster a Culture of Innovation

Creating a culture that values innovation and encourages risk-taking is vital for effective leadership. Leaders should promote an environment where team members feel empowered to take risks, experiment, and explore new ideas. Providing support, resources, and recognition for innovative efforts can drive creativity and enhance overall performance.

4. Enhance Decision-Making Skills

Effective risk-taking requires strong decision-making skills. Leaders should work on enhancing their ability to analyze risks, evaluate potential outcomes, and make informed decisions. This involves gathering relevant information, considering different perspectives, and weighing the potential impact of their choices.

5. Practice Transparent Communication

Clear and transparent communication is key to managing risk and responsibility in leadership. Leaders should focus on communicating their decisions, rationale, and expectations effectively. Engaging in open dialogue with team members helps build trust, align efforts, and ensure that everyone is on the same page.

Chapter 13: MASTERING THE ART OF RISK

Risk is an inherent part of life, influencing personal decisions, professional endeavors, and everything in between. Mastering the art of risk involves not only understanding its complexities but also developing the skills and mindset to navigate uncertainty with confidence and strategic intent. This concluding chapter synthesizes the lessons learned throughout the book, offering a comprehensive guide to mastering risk in various aspects of life and turning uncertainty into opportunity.

Risk is often misunderstood as a mere gamble or chance, but it is far more nuanced. At its core, risk involves the possibility of loss or gain in a situation characterized by uncertainty. Recognizing this fundamental truth is crucial for mastering risk. Risk is not an enemy to be avoided but a dynamic force that, when managed skillfully, can lead to significant rewards.

The essence of risk lies in its dual nature: it encompasses both potential dangers and opportunities. Successful risk management involves acknowledging this duality and developing a balanced approach that allows you to navigate risks effectively while maximizing potential rewards.

The Intersection of Risk and Opportunity

1. Evaluating Risks with a Strategic Lens

Mastering the art of risk begins with a strategic evaluation of potential risks and rewards. This involves a thorough analysis of the situation, understanding the potential impact of different outcomes, and aligning risks with long-term goals. Strategic risk evaluation requires a clear vision, informed decision-making, and a willingness to embrace uncertainty.

A strategic approach to risk involves several key steps:

- Define Objectives: Clearly articulate your goals and desired outcomes. Understanding what you aim to achieve helps in assessing whether the risks you're considering align with your objectives.
- Identify Risks: Recognize and list potential risks associated with your decision or action. This includes both internal and external factors that could influence the outcome.

- Analyze Impact: Evaluate the potential impact of each risk, considering both the likelihood of occurrence and the severity of consequences.
- Develop Mitigation Strategies: Create plans to manage and mitigate identified risks. This includes developing contingency plans and preparing for potential setbacks.

2. Turning Risk into Opportunity

Risk inherently carries the potential for opportunity. Mastering risk involves recognizing and seizing opportunities that arise from uncertain situations. By adopting a proactive mindset and focusing on potential benefits, you can transform risk into a powerful tool for growth and innovation.

Turning risk into opportunity involves:

- Embracing Uncertainty: Rather than fearing uncertainty, view it as a chance to explore new possibilities. Embrace the unknown with curiosity and a willingness to experiment.
- Leveraging Strengths: Utilize your strengths and resources to capitalize on opportunities that arise from risk. Leverage your skills, knowledge, and network to navigate challenges and pursue new ventures.

- Adapting to Change: Be flexible and adaptable in the face of changing circumstances. Embracing change and adjusting your approach as needed allows you to turn unexpected challenges into opportunities for growth.

Developing a Risk-Taking Mindset

1. Cultivating Confidence and Resilience

A key aspect of mastering risk is developing the confidence and resilience to face uncertainty. Confidence is built through experience, knowledge, and a positive mindset. Resilience allows you to bounce back from setbacks and continue pursuing your goals despite challenges.

To cultivate confidence and resilience:

- Gain Experience: Build confidence by gaining experience in managing risk and navigating uncertainty. Each risk-taking experience contributes to your growth and ability to handle future challenges.
- Learn from Failure: Embrace failure as a learning opportunity. Analyze what went wrong, identify lessons learned, and apply those insights to future endeavors.

- Practice Positive Thinking: Maintain a positive and proactive mindset. Focus on potential outcomes and opportunities rather than dwelling on potential failures.

2. Building a Support Network

Having a support network is essential for mastering risk. Surrounding yourself with individuals who provide guidance, encouragement, and diverse perspectives can enhance your ability to manage and embrace risk effectively.

Building a support network involves:

- Seeking Mentorship: Find mentors who have experience in managing risk and can offer valuable advice and support. Learning from their experiences can provide valuable insights and guidance.
- Networking: Connect with others who share similar goals and interests. Building relationships with like-minded individuals can offer support, collaboration opportunities, and diverse perspectives on risk management.
- Engaging with Peers: Share experiences and insights with peers who are also navigating risk. Collaborative discussions and mutual support can enhance your ability to manage risk effectively.

Implementing Risk Management Strategies

1. Developing a Comprehensive Risk Management Plan

A well-developed risk management plan is crucial for navigating risk effectively. This plan outlines your approach to identifying, assessing, and managing risks, providing a structured framework for decision-making and action.

A comprehensive risk management plan includes:

- Risk Identification: Continuously monitor and identify potential risks associated with your goals and activities. Stay vigilant and proactive in recognizing emerging risks.
- Risk Assessment: Evaluate the potential impact and likelihood of identified risks. Prioritize risks based on their significance and potential consequences.
- Mitigation Strategies: Develop and implement strategies to mitigate and manage identified risks. This includes contingency planning, diversification, and risk-sharing approaches.
- Monitoring and Review: Regularly review and update your risk management plan to ensure its effectiveness. Monitor changes in the risk environment and adjust your strategies as needed.

2. Utilizing Risk Tools and Techniques

Several tools and techniques can enhance your ability to manage risk effectively. These include:

- Scenario Analysis: Conduct scenario analysis to assess potential outcomes and impacts of different risk scenarios. This technique helps in understanding the range of possible outcomes and preparing for various contingencies.
- Diversification: Spread your risk by diversifying your investments, activities, or ventures. Diversification helps reduce the impact of individual risks and enhances overall stability.
- Contingency Planning: Develop contingency plans to address potential risks and setbacks. Having predefined actions in place ensures that you are prepared for unexpected challenges.

Embracing Risk for Personal Growth

1. Stepping Out of Your Comfort Zone

Personal growth often requires stepping out of your comfort zone and embracing new challenges. Mastering risk involves pushing beyond familiar boundaries and exploring unfamiliar territories. This willingness to take risks can lead to personal development, increased self-confidence, and expanded horizons.

To step out of your comfort zone:

- Set Ambitious Goals: Challenge yourself with goals that push you beyond your current capabilities. Ambitious goals encourage you to take risks and pursue new opportunities.
- Embrace New Experiences: Seek out experiences that expose you to new situations and challenges. Embracing novelty and uncertainty fosters personal growth and resilience.
- Reflect and Learn: Regularly reflect on your experiences and learn from them. Analyze what you've gained from stepping out of your comfort zone and how it contributes to your personal development.

2. Balancing Risk and Reward in Personal Life

Balancing risk and reward is essential for personal fulfillment and success. In personal life, this balance involves making informed decisions, setting realistic expectations, and managing potential consequences.

To balance risk and reward in personal life:

- Assess Personal Values: Align your risk-taking with your personal values and priorities. Understanding what matters most to you helps in making decisions that reflect your true desires and goals.
- Evaluate Potential Outcomes: Consider the potential rewards and risks associated with your personal decisions. Weigh the benefits against the potential drawbacks to make informed choices.
- Take Calculated Risks: Approach personal risk-taking with a strategic mindset. Assess the potential impact of your decisions and take risks that align with your long-term goals.

Mastering Risk in Professional Life

1. Risk-Taking in Career Development

Career development often involves taking risks, such as pursuing new opportunities, changing industries, or starting a business. Mastering risk in your career involves making strategic decisions, seizing opportunities, and navigating uncertainties with confidence.

To master risk in career development:

- Explore Career Opportunities: Identify and pursue opportunities that align with your skills, interests, and goals. Embrace career risks that offer the potential for growth and advancement.
- Build Professional Skills: Develop skills and expertise that enhance your ability to manage career risks effectively. Continuous learning and professional development contribute to your success.
- Seek Mentorship and Guidance:** Engage with mentors and advisors who can provide valuable insights and support as you navigate career risks and opportunities.

2. Managing Risk in Business Ventures

For entrepreneurs and business leaders, managing risk is a critical aspect of success. Effective risk management in business involves strategic planning, financial oversight, and operational resilience.

To manage risk in business ventures:

- Develop a Business Plan: Create a comprehensive business plan that outlines your vision, goals, and risk management strategies. A well-developed plan helps guide decision-making and mitigate potential risks.
- Monitor Financial Health: Regularly assess and manage the financial health of your business. Monitor cash flow, expenses, and profitability to ensure financial stability.
- Foster a Risk-Aware Culture: Build a culture within your organization that values risk awareness and proactive management. Encourage employees to identify and address potential risks and contribute to a resilient business environment.

CONCLUSION

As we reach the end of our exploration into the power of risk, it becomes clear that risk is far more than just a concept confined to financial markets or business ventures. It is a fundamental aspect of the human experience that influences every decision we make, every path we choose, and every opportunity we seize. Mastering risk is not merely about navigating potential pitfalls but about understanding and harnessing the inherent power of uncertainty to drive personal and professional growth.

The journey to mastering risk involves recognizing its dual nature: it is both a challenge and an opportunity. The key to successful risk-taking lies in understanding this balance and approaching risk with a strategic mindset. By evaluating risks carefully, embracing uncertainty with resilience, and developing effective risk management strategies, you can turn potential threats into powerful catalysts for growth.

Our exploration began with a fundamental understanding of what risk truly means, laying the groundwork for appreciating its complexities and the psychological factors influencing our decisions. We then went into the delicate balance between risk and reward, highlighting how calculated risks can lead to significant gains. We delved into the psychology of risk-taking, examining how emotions such as fear and excitement shape our decisions and how managing these emotions is crucial for effective risk-taking.

We distinguished between calculated and reckless risk, providing insights into how to make informed decisions while avoiding impulsive actions. We also addressed the role of uncertainty in risk-taking, demonstrating how embracing the unknown can unlock new opportunities and drive innovation.

The book further explored how risk manifests in various domains, from business and entrepreneurship to personal growth and relationships. We examined the importance of managing financial risk and how risk can be a powerful tool for personal development. We also discussed the cost of avoiding risk, emphasizing how playing it too safe can lead to stagnation and missed opportunities.

Mastering the art of risk is a multifaceted endeavor that requires a deep understanding of risk dynamics, strategic decision-making, and personal growth. By embracing risk as a powerful tool for opportunity, cultivating a risk-taking mindset, and implementing effective risk management strategies, you can navigate uncertainty with confidence and achieve remarkable results.

The journey to mastering risk involves continuous learning, self-reflection, and a willingness to step beyond the familiar. As you apply the lessons from this book to your personal and professional life, remember that risk is not a barrier but a gateway to growth, innovation, and success. Embrace risk with a strategic approach, harness its potential, and turn uncertainty into opportunity.

Mastering the art of risk positions you to thrive in a dynamic and ever-changing world. Embrace the challenges, seize the opportunities, and navigate the uncertainties with confidence and resilience. The mastery of risk is not just about achieving specific goals but about cultivating a mindset that embraces the unknown and transforms it into a catalyst for extraordinary success.

As we conclude this journey, it is important to remember that mastering risk is an ongoing process. It requires continuous learning, adaptation, and a willingness to confront the unknown with confidence. Embracing risk with a strategic and informed approach allows you to harness its power to drive success and achieve extraordinary results.

In the end, the art of risk is about more than just making decisions; it is about shaping your destiny and transforming uncertainty into opportunity. By applying the insights and strategies discussed throughout this book, you can navigate the complexities of risk with a renewed sense of purpose and clarity.

References

1. Kahneman, D., & Tversky, A. (1979). *Prospect Theory: An Analysis of Decision Under Risk.* Econometrica, 47(2), 263–292.
   This seminal paper explores the decision-making process under conditions of risk and uncertainty.

2. Covey, S. R. (1989). *The 7 Habits of Highly Effective People: Powerful Lessons in Personal Change.* Simon & Schuster.
   Offers insights into personal growth, leadership, and calculated risk-taking.

3. Knight, F. H. (1921). *Risk, Uncertainty, and Profit.* Houghton Mifflin.
   An essential resource for understanding the fundamental differences between risk and uncertainty in economic contexts.

4. Taleb, N. N. (2007). *The Black Swan: The Impact of the Highly Improbable.* Random House.
   Discusses the role of uncertainty and rare events in shaping risk and reward.

5. Covello, V. T., & Merkhofer, M. W. (1993). *Risk Assessment Methods: Approaches for Assessing Health and Environmental Risks.* Springer Science+Business Media.
   Explores structured approaches to managing and mitigating risk.

6. Cialdini, R. B. (2001). *Influence: The Psychology of Persuasion.* Harper Business.
   Explains psychological triggers that drive risk-taking behaviors in decision-making.

7. Sarasvathy, S. D. (2001). *Causation and Effectuation: Toward a Theoretical Shift from Economic Inevitability to Entrepreneurial Contingency.* Academy of Management Review, 26(2), 243–263.
   Highlights entrepreneurial approaches to balancing risk and reward.

8. Pink, D. H. (2009). *Drive: The Surprising Truth About What Motivates Us.* Riverhead Books.
   Investigates intrinsic motivation, personal growth, and risk-taking in achieving goals.

9. Sinek, S. (2014). *Leaders Eat Last: Why Some Teams Pull Together and Others Don't*. Portfolio.
   Examines leadership risk-taking and the role of trust in managing uncertainty.

10. Sunstein, C. R. (2009). *The Laws of Fear: Beyond the Precautionary Principle*. Cambridge University Press.
    A detailed discussion of the societal and psychological cost of avoiding risk.

11. Bernstein, P. L. (1996). *Against the Gods: The Remarkable Story of Risk*. Wiley.
    A historical perspective on the development of risk management and its impact on society.

12. Drucker, P. F. (1985). *Innovation and Entrepreneurship: Practice and Principles*. Harper Business.
    Provides insights into the risks and rewards in entrepreneurship and innovation.

13. Raiffa, H., & Schlaifer, R. (1961). *Applied Statistical Decision Theory*. Harvard University Press.
    Focuses on decision-making frameworks and statistical methods for calculating risks.

14. Dweck, C. S. (2006). *Mindset: The New Psychology of Success*. Random House.
Explores the mindset required for taking risks and achieving personal growth.

15. Goleman, D. (1998). *Working with Emotional Intelligence*. Bantam Books.
Discusses the emotional aspects of risk-taking in relationships and leadership.

16. McKinsey & Company. (2019). *Risk and Resilience: Managing Volatility in a Digital World*.
A business-focused exploration of managing risks in uncertain environments.

17. Gigerenzer, G. (2002). *Reckoning with Risk: Learning to Live with Uncertainty*. Penguin Books.
A practical guide to understanding and dealing with everyday risks.

18. Robbins, A. (1991). *Awaken the Giant Within: How to Take Immediate Control of Your Mental, Emotional, Physical, and Financial Destiny!* Simon & Schuster.
Motivational insights into taking calculated risks for personal and financial success.

19. HBR Editors. (2018). *HBR Guide to Making Smarter, Riskier Decisions*. Harvard Business Review Press. Offers strategies and tools for mitigating risk and making informed decisions.

20. Heath, C., & Heath, D. (2010). *Switch: How to Change Things When Change Is Hard*. Broadway Books. Examines the psychological barriers to risk and the tools to overcome them.

About the Author

Lucas D. Harrington is a dynamic thought leader, entrepreneur, and strategist with a passion for uncovering the hidden opportunities that lie within risk. With over two decades of experience in business consultancy and financial risk management, Lucas has helped countless individuals and organizations master the delicate balance between uncertainty and reward. A sought-after speaker and mentor, he specializes in empowering readers to take calculated risks that lead to transformative growth.

An advocate for lifelong learning, Lucas holds degrees in psychology and business administration, blending insights into human behavior with practical strategies for success. His engaging writing style and actionable advice have made his books a favorite among professionals, entrepreneurs, and anyone seeking to navigate life's uncertainties with confidence and purpose.

When not writing or consulting, Lucas enjoys hiking, chess, and exploring new cultures, drawing inspiration from life's diverse landscapes to fuel his work. Through his books, he continues to inspire others to embrace the art of risk as a pathway to extraordinary achievements.

Disclaimer:

The information presented in this book is for educational and informational purposes only and is not intended as professional advice. The author and publisher have made every effort to ensure the accuracy of the information; however, they assume no responsibility for errors, omissions, or any outcomes resulting from the application of the contents. Readers are encouraged to consult with a qualified professional for specific advice tailored to their situation.

All opinions expressed are those of the author and do not reflect the views of any affiliated organizations. The reader assumes all risks for the use of the material provided in this book. The author and publisher disclaim any liability for direct or indirect consequences arising from the use or interpretation of the information.

All rights reserved. No part of this book may be reproduced, distributed, or transmitted in any form without prior written permission from the author or publisher, except in the case of brief quotations used in reviews.

Copyright

© **2024 by Lucas D. Harrington**
All rights reserved.

No part of this book may be reproduced, distributed, or transmitted in any form or by any means, including photocopying, recording, or other electronic or mechanical methods, without the prior written permission of the publisher, except in the case of brief quotations embodied in critical reviews and certain other noncommercial uses permitted by copyright law.

This book is a work of fiction/nonfiction. Names, characters, places, and incidents are products of the author's imagination or used fictitiously. Any resemblance to actual events, locales, or persons, living or dead, is purely coincidental.

Legal Notice

This book is for informational and educational purposes only. While the author and publisher have made every effort to provide accurate and up-to-date information, they assume no responsibility for any errors, inaccuracies, or omissions. Any reliance placed on the information in this book is strictly at the reader's discretion and risk.

The content is not intended to replace professional advice, including but not limited to medical, legal, financial, or other professional services. Readers should consult with an appropriate professional for specific guidance related to their unique circumstances.

All trademarks, product names, and company names mentioned herein are the property of their respective owners. Their inclusion does not imply endorsement, affiliation, or sponsorship. Unauthorized reproduction, distribution, or transmission of this publication in any form is prohibited without prior written consent from the author or publisher.

By reading this book, you agree to indemnify and hold harmless the author, publisher, and any affiliated parties from and against all claims, liabilities, losses, or damages resulting from your use of the information provided.

www.ingramcontent.com/pod-product-compliance
Lightning Source LLC
Chambersburg PA
CBHW071554220526
45469CB00003B/1014

Copyright © 2024 Pew 13, LLC

All rights reserved

The characters and events portrayed in this book are fictitious. Any similarity to real persons, living or dead, is coincidental and not intended by the author.

No part of this book may be reproduced, or stored in a retrieval system, or transmitted in any form or by any means, electronic, mechanical, photocopying, recording, or otherwise, without express written permission of the publisher.

ISBN-13: 9798301564383
ISBN-10: 1477123456

Cover design by: Timothy Hunter
Library of Congress Control Number: 2018675309
Printed in the United States of America